I0706891

Gaslighting the
BLACK WIDOW

KAREN KELLOCK PH.D.

**Manual for
Superior Men**

**A complete theory based on Einstein physics,
Political Psychology, Systems Theory
and Archetypal Psychiatry.**

FORMULA

**All success attraction
All disease obstruction
All recovery elimination**

**You must fast on all three
OBSTRUCTIONS:
People
Habit
Food**

GASLIGHTING THE BLACK WIDOW

He was mesmerized by her beauty and poise but after he tested her she lost her power and he was annoyed. When he shifts into devaluation a beautiful woman becomes the black widow spider syndrome.   Learning self-love is actually separating from users blocking power from above. First they love then devalue you after saying you were great. You're so sensitive to his moods you need separation from trauma bonds/bad dudes. Now it all falls together in a whole new view.

GASLIGHTING EXPLAINED

Born clear, we mal-adapt to a severe undertow which says we're not a king/queen but trash/low.

It's slave consciousness for women: acting like they own you or you're indebted to them.

A queen will not be pushed beyond her limits. That's the difference between her and the rest.

LOW AND HIGH END WOMEN

Below average women live without any destination in mind nor do they know who/why they are, aye.

They're not clear on what they deserve altho' they may feel entitled from a false narrative.

Pushing her beyond her limits is how he gets his hooks into her sometimes for permanence.

Pushing beyond her limits makes her lose all control so she's under his rule going way low.

What indicates a queen? One who has learned from her lessons and knows her limitations.

This queen has one big limitation: you're not gonna be dropping in or bringing a buncha friends.

Due to my high walls I can't let a narcissist in the house because every boundary they bust.

Though it's your house he will not abide your boundaries and even see them as treachery.

Tho' it's your space he sees your boundaries as the arrogant lines of a bitch see.

GASLIGHTING EXPLAINED

For there's a severe undertow and it's maintained by creeps in your house, so lock em out.

FIRST THEY LOVEBOMB

First they lovebomb and then they push your boundaries til they no longer exist: the narcissists.

Becoming aware of narcissist tactics help us to heal. As cobwebs lift we can finally feel.

A fool is easily separated from his money and leaves things out in rain or he loses em see.

Ghosts in the machine like systemic racism is blamed even when the city council is all black men.

They used to eat to work but now it's a whole addictive thing in itself. The cure: love God first.

Your "prime" is any day you're above ground. Learn to laugh at ageist remarks and be renowned.

Make him lose significance in your life and stop telling yourself stories like future marriage.

REPENTANCE CHANGES MEMORY

With repentance God changes memory. He doesn't want His kid seen in a bad light surely.

The Christian is not condemned. God doesn't want his children to be viewed thru a past lens.

He was hot and heavy for her 'til someone put her down then he dropped her as a clown.

Don't waste time if they don't have a burning desire for you. Don't pursue to avoid rejection too.

GASLIGHTING EXPLAINED

She loves her new dress intensely then when someone bashes it she tosses it in disgust see.

We all have a unique path. Mine was living in a ghost town for 26 years learning about psychopaths.

When you finally seek wellness you lose all curiosity about the object of your addiction see.

When complete the Creative Act acts as a magnet to the predestined link and I'm waiting for it.

EVIL CHANGES THEIR LOOKS

When the devil's using em they look so strong but then the next day they're suddenly mowed down.

Malignant narcissism: psychopathy without guilt/conscience or Machiavellian: exploitive/sadistic.

If it's highs and lows, if he gives you nothing but emotional vacillation, drop him.

I remember that feeling in the gut--the solar plexus--and it's not worth it. Heartpain, forget it.

See your down periood as a bootcamp or reform school. It was necessary, from fool to cool.

You have every right to fear violence of an immature friend after your mature rejection.

When the hedge is down you're blamed for everything. The devil is a false accuser see.

I got so used to being blamed for everything I just accepted it and eventually caved in.

When the hedge is down you're seen in a bad light and then you're easily scapegoated, aye.

GASLIGHTING EXPLAINED

To hell with starvation and bedlam, you're narcissistically worried over what someone said.

People are being killed and you have grudges over what someone said: get the right perspective.

Making mountains out of hills when the ego's been hurt: let it go by seeing this first.

Stay mute and let your work speak for you. It's pure and perfect tho' you weren't always Sue.

SATAN'S A LIAR AND AN ACCUSER

The devil is a liar and accuser. Be ready for this for it's most important you hold your temper.

You got into that mess from not knowing any better so don't sweat the lesson tho' it hurt sister.

Acting like they own you or you owe them an explanation: it's very evident in this generation.

They're entitled to your life cuz you're "friends" but you're not, you're mere acquaintances.

Like the "dumb blond" there are unfortunate characterizations of people, often very evil.

Silly women are below average and laden with sins. They just wanna wake up cute, amen.

Silly women have diverse lusts and are taken in by wicked men creeping into her house.

She attracts unscrupulous men while always learning but never coming to the truth of sin.

You can only write when ready to write then it all pours out day and night so wait then alight.

GASLIGHTING EXPLAINED

They **CREEP** in. The bored and lonely don't call first because they know you'd resist.

As all intellectuals you can't stand surprises. It's appointment only from now on/no compromises.

The communist spirit translates to social culture which means hangout culture/we're all superior.

DON'T LET EM STEAL YOUR TIME

Don't let em steal your time, your greatest asset even beyond money. Wall off the bored and lonely!

If you don't set and rigidly maintain boundaries you'll be invaded naturally by the social see.

They're bored and lonely cuz schools don't encourage kids to get into their own thing see.

It's all **SOCIAL, SOCIAL, SOCIAL** and I thought I'd lost my mind in the chaotic public school.

Mom pushed me to "socialize" with the girl next to me tho' I didn't know her. What a bummer.

The false church stresses social pot lucks and other get togethers, the true church studies verses etc.

They act like social avoidance means you hate God. The deacons are Mr. and Mrs. Social Charm.

We need solitude to lead the tribe and to overcome the undertow to self-esteem/greatness, aye.

Just as Jesus had to escape the multitudes you know, tho' He felt compassion and sorrow.

The bored and lonely want your time for **THEM**. For your destiny there is no consideration.

GASLIGHTING EXPLAINED

For I know my limitations: if I conform to you I'll be frazzled and may even fall into addiction.

I'm not gonna conform to you and the demons in your kids. A queen is CLEAR and sees the twits.

A queen marries and is degraded by the step kids. Due to the undertow she loses all charisma

THE STEPMOTHER SYNDROME

There's an undertow: Hold Your Head Up High. Expect the low: Be ready to say bye bye.

I caved into the step kids and the contagion of madness quickly ensued, I'll never forget this.

The low don't learn from lessons [same old patterns] and are unaware of limitations so suffer invasion.

The world [run by Satan] seeks to block your destiny see: your armor is your boundaries.

Though happily married his kids ripped us apart and my reputation fell into ill fame/ignominy.

The queen must be strong to withstand these worldly forces seeking to divide her from husband.

To deal with stepchildren study abnormal and developmental psychology and Systems Theory.

The crushed queen lets the same old types in again and again, never learning her lessons.

Know and abide your limitations, don't tolerate anything like the below average women.

For you were made for a purpose and Satan's world of "social" seeks to block all this.

GASLIGHTING EXPLAINED

I tried being their pal, they took advantage. I tried being a disciplinarian, they went on a rampage.

The Evil Stepmother Syndrome is where a nice lady becomes a witch from fairytale projections.

EAT FOR ERRANDS NOT ENTERTAINMENT

Eat to get the jobs done and to run your errands. Don't eat as your form of entertainment.

I can't imagine eating breakfast/lunch/dinner, it seems insane. It's breakfast-only for the saints.

When I do eat it's five minutes to make tacos then back up to the office for 24 hours.

I see three meals as a waste of time, money and digestive energy: go breakfast-only.

If you wanna look like a god eat God's food or look like the herd where processed is preferred.

Ice Cream Diet: This is sugar for glucose energy and fat for satiety for 24 hours hunger free.

The cancel mob bans speakers they don't agree with, unapproved words or apathy re: perceived injustices.

Anyone in the racial equity cult must be treated with anathema if he ever disputes it much.

Gaslighting the

BLACK WIDOW

STOCKHOLM SYNDROME/TRAUMA BONDS
BIOCHEMICAL ADDICTION TO HIM
NO CONTACT IS THE ONLY WAY
DON'T COUNT ON CIVILITY
GET A SUPPORT SYSTEM NOW
THE AGING NARCISSIST
HEALTHY AGING
BLACK WIDOW SYNDROME
HANKERING FOR DISCARDERS
LOVEBOMBING THEN DISCARDING
SEE THE CYCLES, BE RELIEVED
ALL NARCISSISTS ARE SADISTS
THE PARENTS MAY SEEM IDEAL
GO NO-CONTACT!
SEEKING NURTURANCE FROM BETRAYAL SOURCE
NOT BEING LOVED IS BETRAYAL
DON'T TAKE BACK DISRESPECTERS
PULLING THE RUG OUT
VICTIM BECOMES BLACK WIDOW SPIDER
CHIPPING AWAY AT IDENTITY

Gaslighting the BLACK WIDOW

Gaslighting the **BLACK WIDOW**

I'm at my highest game, my apex--and I'm to be bogged down by your silliness? Not a chance.

The flying monkeys are enablers of the abuse but they are also complicit, later don't forget this.

They seem to be oblivious with reality and wouldn't know the truth if it laid em flat, truly.

Give up visions of family reunion cuz for most it probably won't happen, they aren't changin'.

It is against the law in most states to stalk you, bully you, mob you or physically threaten you.

These enablers are equally as lethal as the malignant narcissist, robots without common sense.

STOCKHOLM SYNDROME/TRAUMA BONDS

Trauma bonds are toxic relationships between abuser and victim, even a hostage/kidnap situation.

It can happen with anyone even a stranger: a trauma bond which is an *emotional* attachment.

These trauma bonds are not healthy but psychologically destructive relationships, always.

These relationships have an unequal power balance, as in the case of an older woman beholden.

When the parent goes from syrupy sweet to seething mad in a minute who knows how to adapt?

Gaslighting the BLACK WIDOW

A narc has a Jeckyl and Hyde personna and you never know when he'll blow so you're stuck below.

The Stockholm Syndrome is the emotional trauma bonding of victim with abuser alone.

There are moments when they're very nice then many when there's great cruelty, yikes.

They alternate between hate and love--kindness and cruelty--and that's the sign of trauma bond.

It's this confusion of sick cycles--sickly cyclicity--that's that addicting thing to the trauma victim.

The smallest accident could bring a blowup and usually you don't know why, that's just your house.

Addicted to their abuser? Wow that's heavy stuff, can that be true? Do your research to confirm.

Not putting the shame and blame on the abuser is part of the trauma bond as the victim cowers.

BIOCHEMICAL ADDICTION TO HIM

Due to the rush of the stress hormone cortisol you could be addicted biochemically to them all.

One chemical dopamine can trigger the reward center making you think you love your abuser.

Justifying/making excuses for narcissists is a sign of trauma bonds enabling these family lunatics.

It could be 85% abusive and 15% nice and the victim would see it as equal, excusing his vice.

Your gut instinct alerting you to danger is right-on and must be heeded. It just doesn't feel right see.

NO CONTACT IS THE ONLY WAY

Disengage from both the narc and his monkeys. Do not explain a thing just do this immediately.

They don't care how you feel nor understand you. They will never relate and will deny everything too.

The point is taking your power back--getting back in the driver's seat--and that's thru no-contact.

No-contact is the key to the healing journey and the only way to move forward successfully.

If you decide instead to stay do not be surprised when your life spirals outa control/hell to pay.

DON'T COUNT ON CIVILITY

She just hated me and didn't want to even try to understand me. We can't count on civility.

You say you're stressed out and going insane. But you choose to stay in that matrix anyway?

Release all hope of reconciliation or their change. Step back to make new decisions/re-arrange.

This radical rearrangement on your part will disarm the flying monkeys in this soul-crushing war.

Seek support. The narc and her monkeys want you isolated and alone but your star has shone.

Life is a Cinderella Syndrome. Early trauma and isolation then a saving prince comes along.

Completely disconnect and go cold on the system as though you never knew them, The End.

Suddenly she realized her mother had been gossiping about her all along, even to strangers.

When suddenly the whole system comes down on you you gotta have one friend/support too.

The terror when they all believe the narcissist smear campaign and you've not one friend ok.

GET A SUPPORT SYSTEM NOW

While disengaging from this sick system focus on new supports for your emotional wellness hon'.

The less you communicate with them the better off you are. Go no-contact with every single player.

By getting back in contact [with the narc and her monkeys] you could have an intense setback.

I'm not gonna expend the negative energy dealing with all that. Ghosts from the past, egotists.

Self-care is crucial. Building up your support system, educating yourself about abuse cycles.

It took a lifetime to learn healthy boundaries and the consequences of not doing so/being free.

The best way to empower ourselves is to walk away from disempowering relationships ok.

THE AGING NARCISSIST

There is no hope a malignant narcissist will change. Hope obstructs your new life so joyous.

As he ages his devices for supply become more caricatured and it's quite pathetic for sure.

Gaslighting the BLACK WIDOW

As his sources dry up he faces his true self covered up while the false self loses all its magic.

Narcs use charm, looks, etc. to gain supply and power over others so when those go it's a crisis.

Most of us know happiness comes from within but not so with the narcissist, it's outer things.

Their happiness is strictly determined by how much supply they get on a day to day basis.

HEALTHY AGING

Healthy aging is taking stock in our accomplishments, feeling gratitude, enjoying naps afternoons.

Healthy aging is feeling grateful to fall outa structure, to be outa the jungle, to not need approval.

Aging for normal people is maturity and enjoying the fruits of labor not continuing as an actor.

Aging means taking some time off and slowing down, enjoying the view and tea time too.

But narcs have lived in a false reality where they are the star of the movie and the best of all see.

He is the one and only power, one who everyone else is jealous of--his self-created world of Oz.

With age he's faced with realities that do not align with his false self vision and his panic deepens.

Narcs want everyone to mirror back how special they are and with age that's gone, he's no star.

As they age the reflection they get back--in terms of narcissistic supply--declines or goes black.

Gaslighting the BLACK WIDOW

Panic triggers the true self underlying the false one. It feels deeply inferior & flawed/no fun.

They will turn into the most severe and horrendous version of their worst self, it's very sad.

The narc isn't interested in any other version of reality than the false one they've created.

When this created version of the narcissistic self is threatened it's a life or death situation.

Loss of allure is beyond agonizing to them, experiencing the loss of control never encountered before.

BLACK WIDOW SYNDROME

He was mesmerized by her beauty and poise but after he tested her she lost her power and he was annoyed.

When he shifts into devaluation a beautiful woman becomes the black widow spider syndrome.

Girl, if you're smart but without a solid sense of self you're gonna be gaslighted constantly into the Black Widow Spider.

Allowing someone to determine her reality chips away at her identity as she becomes the *Black Widow Spider.*

Learning to self-love is actually learning how to separate from users sucking the life right outa you.

Suddenly your bubble is popped about somebody. Suddenly a success not a victim of nobodies.

He popped my bubble about him and I lost respect for him. What a sad sight it is: depedestalization.

HANKERING FOR DISCARDERS

Once outa jail why go back to visit the vicious jail guards? But that's what we do, hankering for discarders.

Your desire for a jerk reflects the tenacity of the original trauma, a broken bond you're seeking to correct/a curse.

What's with all your rules and regulations? Don't wear this or that, don't be yourself be more like me, crap.

Why do you say "grow up--don't wear beanies"? They keep our head warm and it's what you're wearing.

Going to their page is like knocking on their door then getting their crap thrown in your face.

Anyone who tells you not to do something when it's the very thing he's doing is the King of Sorrow.

LOVEBOMBING THEN DISCARDING

If one needs another to feel whole it's a breeding ground for idealization and love-bombing, a no-no.

Once you're love-bombed and bonded to that person he instantly starts the discard phase of rejection.

Love-bombing fills the trauma-bonded with joy and good feelings, naturally--a euphoria, you're loved finally.

They get you to the highest point then pop your bubble to experience the elation of you falling into trouble.

The shrewd man mirrors your values and character till you fall in love with yourself, then he discards fast.

While you're falling he's idealizing someone else cuz he's always gotta keep it going, he's always doing it.

If a weakness to flattery--needing to hear it--you're ready supply for the narc who will deflate you quickly.

Believing in fairy tales or magical thinking is open feed for the narcissist cuz it's ALL a big fantasy twist.

He just wants her to "fall" in love then he instantly discards and this is his major matrix dove.

The false love of the narcissist is MEANT to take you down so don't fall for it and stay grounded.

I was innocent tho' trauma bonded and he faked his way in then pulled the rug out/I was confounded.

It was a war--you know what happens in wartime now. Your war was between good and evil's undertow.

SEE THE CYCLES, BE RELIEVED

See the CYCLES in these systems--that is true wisdom. Just when things are good, expect bedlam.

A child raised in pain becomes cued-up for it. This is the masochist who actually enjoys it--don't be this.

No Contact means you don't give em your pain--thinking as a masochist that love and pain are the same.

Be patient as you rewire your brain--away from thinking that love and pain are one and the same.

See creeps for what they really are and realize you've been confiding your hurts and they've enjoyed it large.

They feel good when you're being ostracized. They get off on any humiliation cutting you down to size.

Your family is a shark tank and it's fun and relieving to realize this. Just wait, they'll all get theirs.

They love your failures/making you feel inadequate/old. The answer is to get out of the system and be bold.

Gaslighting the BLACK WIDOW

Understand what you're dealing with cuz it's **NOT** a good thing but psycho devastating--they are cruelians.

Other things in life are so much better. You never need to deal with types you knew when you were younger.

If you're a black sheep, know they love ostracizing and pushing it in your face. Block em fast, start anew Ace!

ALL NARCISSISTS ARE SADISTS

REALIZE above all that narcissists are sadists. You don't need any more of this--start living with optimists.

Recap: Stop sharing your pain with people who enjoy it. Become aware of those you never suspected.

It's hard to find out someone you cared about or knew was always deliberately trying to destroy you.

Exploitive manipulators work in covertly subtle ways. Nothing's obvious, it's a secret behind a mask.

Unmet dependency needs as a kid means we have an open hole of toxic shame, ready for narcs to come in.

You're open, with no sense of self-worth and the exploiters flow in taking advantage of these gaps in your map.

You needed to be accepted, nurtured and cared for and the narc attracts in to get the supply you're ready for.

Holes of Shame: You don't know who you are, what you deserve or how you should be treated. Fresh meat.

The narc attracts thru these dependency needs to get his supply and **THAT'S** why it's so covert, so sly.

When they listen it's only to things they prefer but you don't notice--not knowing you've a right to be heard.

Gaslighting the BLACK WIDOW

Though your alarm system is a siren around this guy, you don't listen to it or realize the imminent tragedy.

If everything you think is stupid and everything you do is worthless you won't listen to yourself--but do this.

It's so covert it looks innocent. Bystanders witnessing the family interactions would see nothing evident.

THE PARENTS MAY SEEM IDEAL

The parents may seem like the ideal mother and father. While the child is being destroyed, no one's aware.

Their soul is being murdered one manipulative move at a time. Jenna Ryan

Still trying to get their unmet needs they grow up in a world of narcissists hunting for fresh meat.

Still trying to prove themselves and get back lost love they'll do anything for approval from narcs.

Where will they go? Repetition compulsion: right into the arms of exploiters just like their parents again.

The narc will **MEET THOSE NEEDS** [get their hooks in] then turn around and walk away, entirely sadistically.

Once under their control they play with you as a cat does a mouse. Nice one day and horrible the next.

Whenever you don't feel well about yourself or feel psychic pain--look around at your relationships, just sayin'

Because it's so covert you can't put your finger on it. These people are my friends, aren't they? NOT

GO NO-CONTACT!

The minute you find out who's abusing you covertly you gotta cut em out. Instantly you go **NO CONTACT**.

Gaslighting the BLACK WIDOW

Don't fall in love with a narc thinking it will be different for it's a bottomless cavern, another narc snake-pit.

What makes man human? The ability to see signs symbolically and symbols significantly. Karl Pribram

That's synchronicity: watching for miracles like a cat watches a mouse hole. Karl Jung

If you went back it wouldn't be the same. It wasn't those people it was a drama played out, era-driven.

They'll come miles to bury you/collect what's left but won't take a step to support you alive: Go No Contact.

You won't notice people are influencing you until it's too late. It works like that--nip it in the bud, be great.

Hangout with them to become a boring normal person who's "very nice" but inwardly filled with vice.

You were passionate, creative, bold and truthful. Now cuza your associates your boring, nice, weak, fullabull.

Now it's too late. The system has changed you. You're now fullabull--it happens like frog in slow boil.

Pick only friends you want to be like. Don't sink into the swill of users bringing you down, go No Contact.

Spend time with people you don't like, you'll adapt and then before you know it be just like them: yikes.

The narcissist mom urges the loner to "be social" and accept everyone no matter how low they go.

They expected me to be open and nice to everyone. Are they kidding? I vet every one of them.

SEEKING NURTURANCE FROM BETRAYAL SOURCE

Seeking nurturance from a betrayal source: this is the stupidest thing I've ever done of course.

The betrayal source is anyone who has broken your boundaries or betrayed your trust.

Someone who doesn't respect who you are, who has cheated on you or broken your heart.

It's dangerous for your soul to let past abusers back into your life. Leak self-esteem, you don't even exist.

It HURTS badly without the internal boundaries necessary to NOT seek nurturance from betrayal sources.

NOT BEING LOVED IS BETRAYAL

Nurture: Seeking something who will make us feel good when we feel bad. Yah, but not from that cad.

Even though they didn't mean to, a parent not giving us the love we needed is classified as betrayal.

It's because they didn't get what THEY needed, but nevertheless it was the cause of what followed.

What else can the dependent child do but not-exist and deny his own needs to maintain the relationship?

We've gotta bond with this PERSON who is being abusive towards us. Talk about cognitive dissonance.

This lays the course of hankering for the betrayal source. Bad people you wanna see anyway: dangerous!

You wanting/nondiscerning bad people indicates you were betrayed as a child, without any doubt.

If you were healthy/loved properly it wouldn't feel right to seek nurturance from a betrayer, your enemy.

Gaslighting the BLACK WIDOW

My boundaries were violated/I was being exploited yet I allowed her in again unaware of the pattern.

We're abused thru the sweet-mean cycle of blow up--calm down--nice again. Don't tolerate this friends.

Adapting to mean vs. nice all day causes an addiction to form and people on the TAKE are not your friends.

DON'T TAKE BACK DISRESPECTERS

Don't text em after a couple of beers and never let em back in your home. Draw that line now, they're DONE.

It's like a slot machine: you keep pulling and it's good or it's bad but the problem is it goes down to your heart.

What happens when you're betrayed when little? Betrayal Blindness--you can't discern the truly hateful.

Letting a disrespecter back in your life always gets worse it never gets better, that's the natural progression.

Taking back a disrespecter is the same as abusing yourself and other victims of that lecher.

We can't stop ourselves when we're not aware that we're not aware and we want what we want right now.

The Betrayal/Trauma Bond is what keeps this sick system running. You keep running back tho' it's abusing.

With Betrayal Blindness you don't notice abuse until the next day you're irritable, angry, depressed, obtuse.

Before running to your betrayal source, stop and listen to your heart. Are you avoiding pain or making it start?

This Pain Tunnel is the root of addiction. It's what causes you to go back and repeat cycles to find the End.

These people deserve to be shut OUT of your life for good, don't even entertain thoughts of accepting hoods.

It's the critical parent that holds this in place where you go back to an abuser since in the past he was nicer.

The abuser starts nice. He doesn't come as the devil so that's what you remember when in big trouble.

They come bearing gifts, flattering and meeting your needs. Then they SWITCH: count on this please.

PULLING THE RUG OUT

On the down slope they slowly/quickly take the rug out from under you--gut aches, always something new.

You choosing an abuser indicates an inner war inside of you--someone who's two-faced and soon blue.

What's inside of you that would cause you to go back to an abuser? Inner work is needed to be sane and clear.

Attraction to an abuser indicates the need for healing, self-love, internal boundaries and addiction therapy.

Recovery: Clean the slate, start over with good habits, block out or compartmentalize that lunatic.

Attraction to unavailable men is really self-abusive, friend.

The worst narcissist is the sweet and nice who is so covert in his bloodletting no ones convinced.

We must heal the shame that binds us or when that mask comes off we're shocked by the lack of kindness.

Trauma blindness means you miss the abuse around you cuz it's COVERT--you don't know how you're hurt.

Gaslighting the BLACK WIDOW

Other gaslighting techniques of lunatics: "I never said that" or "I was just kidding" though you're made frantic.

Why does narcissism include triangulation? So he's sure to end up on top-- making you jealous with em.

If I were you I'd fear the "shit-tests" of narcissists cuz it can be very serious and dangerous, I attest to this.

A "narc harem" is fresh meat in case you bail out. He always has a bevy of em waiting to be called up.

VICTIM BECOMES BLACK WIDOW SPIDER

What creates the Black Widow? Other people and their mean projections/inability to see the other.

Psychology is fast becoming Sociobiology—the study of CONNECTIONS or systems of crazy humans.

What happens to her with this false accusation and calumny? She's the Black Widow Spider [she gets ugly].

It's so impossibly hard for the true victim to be HIT then the hitter going around refusing responsibility for it.

And this has been happening since you were a little child traumatized by being abused AND blamed for it.

I will never forget the frustration of trying to explain to simpletons that I was the victim, not him!

Because his constant pecking away at my identity made me crazy--who'd believe that Black Widow lady?

Withdrawn affection makes a woman ugly while being loved makes her beautiful--that's it in a nutshell.

Withdrawn affection PLUS a monkey army against me stole my beauty completely and I was his meal, see?

His monkey army believes lies so their attacks are vicious. Recover from the narcissist and never forget this.

Jezebel's monkey army comes from phone-work. She's on the horn all day smearing you with bad remarks.

The minute you see him triangulating to get your attention or making you feel less than his harem, get rid of him.

Many men will brag about how many women they've had showing pics of them hand in hand--reject that man.

CHIPPING AWAY AT IDENTITY

"I didn't throw that plate. How dare you accuse me of that--this proves how crazy you are". Narcissist game.

Narcissist is always selfishly making plans whether you like it or not--bringing all their friends into your house.

Triangulation is correlation of narcissism and jealousy-inducing behaviors e.g. like lunging at cute clerks.

The narc whether male or female builds an army ready to attack--these "flying monkeys" are always a fact.

You now realize he's been smearing you the whole time so when you reach out to friends you get **NOTHING**.

The triangulation and flying monkey army is so solid that suddenly it seems her whole world has fallen.

Jezebel also builds a flying monkey army--did it not seem strange her friends attacking you unreasonably?

The narcissist must stay **ABOVE** you as the victim--so his army is **KEY** to maintaining your one-down position.

Behind your back there's a collection of smear campaigns so when it ends it **ALL** blows up in your face.

Gaslighting the BLACK WIDOW

I wasn't even aware of all this going on, though I felt miserable picking up on something all around.

THE SMEAR CAMPAIGN

The smear campaign at the end is inevitable cuz narcs can't just go away--they always end on top that way.

They MUST gaslight [call you crazy] to deflect your objections and always--ALWAYS--play the victim.

If I confirm you're crazy I never have to go inside and "crack the mask" to unravel what's inside of ME.

I was taking a hot bath minding my own business and here came another smear campaign causing shame.

Your friend says "that's not what I heard" and you realize he was talking to her all along. You feel so all alone.

When it all crashes down at the end cuza your "friends" you feel like a little baby crushed in the crib.

Solution: see his triangulation as an energy BALL. Focus on it, it grows. Pull energy from it = away it goes.

RELEASE FOCUS, YOU'RE FREE MISS

Keep talking/focusing and the problem grows. Withdraw energy and it dissipates/shrinks to a mere shadow.

No Contact means them all. Don't follow him on media and ban ALL the frenemies who were part of your fall.

Classic end to all this: As you overcame, the collaborator "friends" never speak to each other again.

They were just little minion-demons whose only connection was jealousy of you, God's great/peculiar champion.

As you deliberately pull attention away from the energy ball, concentrate only on **YOUR** life/have a ball.

RECAP of your new map: **UP** your self-care while you **WITHDRAW** attention from him and his minions.

Never trust "ladies night out" cuz they go to bars and talk against you for centuries of torture--for sure.

A true lady stays in her home protected from the outer but nowadays they can't wait to get to the bars.

When these things come to the surface it's an opportunity to move forward-- e.g. crying jags about the coward...

FAMILY SCAPEGOATS

The scapegoat may have the courage to speak out but is quickly dominated back into submission.

There's unspoken rules in narcissistic families and an emotional pain that's kept hidden.

There's an undercurrent of sibling rivalry as they constantly fight for the parent's love and attention, see?

The narc parent is very threatened by the black sheep, the only one with the courage to expose these creeps.

The scapegoat is very aware of what's going on and sees the truth behind the facade the narc lays out.

The scapegoat feels nothing is ever good enough. With mom happy one day but not the next, it's rough.

If you speak up about how you feel the parent is quick to put you in your place as too sensitive, even cruel.

Despite mood swings/bullying tactics the narc mom relies on the scapegoat to take the blame: facts.

Gaslighting the BLACK WIDOW

REVERSED SOCIAL IMAGES

Anything making a bad impression of the family is his blame while they're seen as very upstanding.

As the parent has chosen YOU to be the bad one she ceases to protect you from their shenanigans.

The sisters/brothers taunt and brutalize the target since this family dynamic is already set up.

"Scapegoat" is specifically relegated to the outspoken intuitive empath, accused of being a liar/lunatic.

The one who sees it will now be getting it as they all gang up. The scapegoat knows all, and writes about it.

"She's mentally ill" or "she loves to exaggerate" and outsiders believe em. I've experienced this fate.

My feminist sister Jane took hold and told Mom she'd scold this dissident witness to a family so brutal and cold.

The scapegoat feels rejected, isolated and alone. NO one understands, she's a stranger in a strange land.

THE SCAPEGOAT ACTS OUT

She feels extremely burdened with all the neglects, wrongdoings and faults so begins to ACT OUT.

By the scapegoat acting out he unknowingly transmutes all this tension in the family dynamic--they need it.

No matter if recognized for excellence, winning a school trophy or straight A's, Jane said "don't believe it".

Everything she did well was minimized, unacknowledged or completely ignored by the cruel feminist sister.

Gaslighting the BLACK WIDOW

I could never meet their standards no matter how good and all praise was giving to Grace, the "golden child"

With Grace, no matter what she did she was always praised. The scapegoat saw this, hurt/amazed.

Golden child has been allocated that role but also objectified--but it's a much easier one, I cried.

I believed what they said about me for decades and my life sunk into Hades as evil broke thru the floodgates.

In adolescence the scapegoats inability to get parental attention means they act out with other sins.

The two evil feminists--Jane the punisher/Grace the golden child--saw themselves as superior with style.

Jane was so hoity-toity she tried to steal scapegoat's husband, bribed with money stolen from Karen.

YOU DON'T EVEN EXIST

As I sunk into despair they forgot I was even there. They gave me a funeral and I didn't have a prayer.

Though sad, the implications in later life were disastrous with constant guilt, shame and resentment.

If any contact is made decades later they're STILL to blame for everything wrong in the family: insane.

By inciting family mobbings against scapegoat it takes the focus away from the real perpetrators: Jane/MOM.

Jane destroyed her husband for not being a liberal like her. She made us all hate him and took his children.

Women can be horrible how they destroy siblings and husbands who disagree with their liberal notions.

Gaslighting the BLACK WIDOW

I will talk about scapegoatism until the day I die. I figure that's why I experienced it along with family LIES.

She had Don declared insane cuz he believed things inane and he was mandatorily drugged/died in the rain.

Grace destroyed our Christian family by bringing a Hindu in cuz Mom had to give up her faith to be "loved" again.

By me accepting my role as the black sheep it allowed the others to feel better about themselves tho' creeps.

The scapegoat then is a very important role when keeping the others seemingly whole, a buncha black souls.

The scapegoat role in dysfunctional families demonstrates HOMEOSTASIS: they keep the system going AS IS.

A good example of Jane types is the sister who advises abortion then blames her and tells everyone.

INTERNALIZING UNFAIR CRITICISMS

As scapegoats internalize unfair criticisms they develop a "harsh inner critic" constantly repeating this setup.

This is so toxic to an impressionable child, I remember the days and nights crying for God to take my life.

The scapegoat struggles with low self-worth and feels deeply inadequate and unlovable, I know it well.

The abandonment anxiety still remains/increases through these times of trying to keep from drowning.

In becoming super-sensitive about seeing the signs of approval/disapproval we gradually lose our minds.

These are just some of the signs of the profound impact that a toxic family dynamic has, and I'm free of it.

Issues with authority, always justifying yourself, overworking, sucking up to prove it, oh my.

I've not re-visited the scapegoat syndrome until today. At first I cried then it brought final relief--hurray.

It was excruciating being blamed tho' I said nothing or misunderstood as bad because I was an anomaly.

I had to constantly prove my worth, an unconscious pattern that paradoxically took me far after this curse.

The victim doesn't realize how powerful these dynamics STILL are--I'm mad as hell writing this sitting here.

ADDICTIONS TO COPE

The unfairly blamed victim may cope with alcohol then go insane with pent-up rage. See? she really is crazy.

I learned to break all these patterns by choosing to behave and think differently. Like a queen, not so nutty.

Choose your battles in mind. Let awareness interrupt when memories unwind. As anger lifts, decide to be kind.

Entering adulthood means acceptance that we may never be friends with the perpetrator, with few exceptions.

The scapegoat truth-teller is unable to tolerate lies and injustice while the others could as accomplices.

Scapegoats gain strength and applause having survived an onslaught of shame and threats from these broads.

I survived the evil flood and was used to being shunned from the rest so gained strength to write/resist.

It's called "transgenerational dysfunction" which for weaker souls means death, illness, addiction, prison.

There are many strengths we do gain if this is our allocated role, and I did for sure with very high goals.

When it comes to the scapegoat-sinner what came first—the chicken or the eggs? Born bad or framed?

GETTING UNSTUCK FROM OLD PARADIGMS

Getting unstuck from old paradigms: because we should always be debunking our repetitious rewinds.

You've seen his blowups covered over, his triangulations with others and his gaslighting of you, a wonder.

We can't collapse into it from fear of what others think about us, leftover childhood shame, whatever it is.

Never trust a slut cuz she'll bring criminals into your house since she attracts narcissists and doesn't know enough.

If in bad relationships you're ignoring red flags. Improving inner guidance system should be your whole bag.

As we heal from narcissistic abuse, finding liars/thieves as they rise to the surface is easy to reject/refuse.

Don't hate these shocks, they are OPPORTUNITIES to flush things out and abolish your blocks.

Self-awareness and self-empathy can definitely help you to survive a narcissistic smear campaign—just sayin'

All narcissists create DRAMA because they get supply from it. This includes dating, work, everything.

Supply, attention = drama. Never allow this with a housekeeper bringing problems in with her!

DON'T AROUSE THEIR ATTENTION

Gaslighting the BLACK WIDOW

If your boss is a narcissist don't give him any reason to come down on you, ever. Watch yourself.

Why? Because you don't want to arouse their attention. You'll be happier to keep that to a minimum.

Don't talk about the narcissist to anyone. I'm talking bad talk though Lord knows you have good reason.

Don't gossip cuz it'll get back and the narcissist boss will hate your guts and you're a fired sad sack.

You wanna stop repetition compulsion and repeating the patterns learned as a child. Awareness is how.

Recovery is a physical thing as new neuropathways replace the old ones. Work new goals/make new friends.

They fake you out so you tell em your stuff until it's too late. They'll use it against you--all your old freight.

Watch out for their fake empathy so you open up about your tragedy. They'll use it as leverage--this is key.

The further you are from the abusive relationship the clearer things become/the more you've had it.

I noticed his one main pattern: Any time I was up he was compelled to pull me down--I didn't trust him.

If I went from happy to miserable, that was his one-up game of which he was never culpable.

NARC THEME SONG: IT WASN'T ME

The theme song of the narcissist is "it wasn't me". Don't argue just get that restraining order/get free.

Narcs lie without thinking, it's part of their one-up game. It makes them less vulnerable to lie-lie-lie, ok?

Gaslighting the BLACK WIDOW

The extreme empath is delicious meat for the narc so assertion training brings escape/takes her far.

Narcs never take accountability for anything, ever. You gotta ignore their words--now you're clever.

You need to know how you attract narcs. Do you overshare? Are you codependent, needy in relationships?

Do you have a low self-esteem problem, did you have a difficult childhood? Know this, you should.

I was so lonely all my life I'd immediately over-share when I'd get an ear--this was a loud siren to abusers.

As he comes in the shark surveys the room. Your empathy is like blood in the water and it means your doom.

YOUTH TEND TO BE NARCISSISTS

Youth tend to be narcissist thinking only of themselves so they do crazy things but I seclude myself.

A woman shouldn't talk to another man than her husband cuz her emotions are triggered and it's not fair.

I had to learn to defend myself living in a tiny cabin on 1000 acres without a fence--that's why I'm smart/not dense.

As long as I was a sweet empath I was taken advantage of constantly--the sharks smelled meat.

Now I see the home--MY home--as sacred and no one gets in here unless thoroughly vetted or forget it.

To think of what I used to put up with makes me sick. We see true reality the further away we get.

Seeing true reality about jerks/Jezebels can pull you back down--see it, laugh at it, understand it now forget it.

Don't pine over it for thirty years like I did. This held me back but also propelled me to work/move on ahead.

PAST MEMORIES ANCHOR YOU DOWN

Life is about progression so why think of things happening before your maturation, so weak you let em all in?

Thinking of the past--when you were weak--acts like little anchors to pull you back to the backseat, effete.

You always had it in you--education/strong foundation--but as a ridiculous weak woman you let THEM in?

I let em in cuz I lost my vision and didn't feel a reason for continued livin' cuz the narcissist said I was nothin'.

Lost vision, lowered self-esteem, blocked creativity, lost confidence = NEEDINESS for anyone even him.

I admire bull dog tenacity, resilience, strength in adversity, fidelity and him protecting the weak, that's me.

Don't worry, rest now before the Tsunami hits. Cuz once they start to sell they ALL will and you're all set.

Since you now KNOW devaluation follows idealization, you can get ready for it and never get hurt again.

DIVORCE

Weakness is giving irresponsible partners second/third chances when they shoulda been gone years back.

Trying to win back a failed relationship is another sign of painful and humiliating low self-esteem, I think.

Every time you take him back the put-downs are worse because everything in these cycles increase.

Gaslighting the BLACK WIDOW

After divorce the confused/hurt may date the wrong people, rush into love and some sleep around.

Post-divorce addictions create their own problems yet seem to remove you from the first, but I wonder.

Divorcees go into isolation or abuse drugs and alcohol but acting out sexually is the most destructive of all.

Divorce shows you who your friends are and you'll see many dump you and go on his side, for sure.

If he does stupid things while drinking like cheating his great life is over cuz the wife created structure.

Even the biggest douche seems a hero when interacting with a woman in a shitty marriage. George Bruno

If she doesn't have sex she doesn't get hurt cuz she's not like a cat scratching at the back door obsessed.

When you came along you flipped her moral compass in a single night--that's how fast truth ignites.

Forgiveness is a budget: you can either have success or remember the mess but you can't have both. Let it go

Total chastity is the only way to not get hurt. Being a lady is the only invulnerability, believe me.

YOU'RE NOT A BOOTIE CALL

Cuz we're unequally yoked--we're more into longterm bonding than they are so get hurt when they discard.

It's degrading, horrible for your self-esteem and your heart. Casual sex is anti-female, a fake, it is dark.

Here he rejected you but you can't move on, constantly stuck in the backstreet wicked trash bin.

Gaslighting the BLACK WIDOW

Women and men have sex differently. Women have attachment hormones that increase vulnerability.

Whenever a woman is someone's "bootie call" she is just re-attaching herself then again breaking it all.

Don't ever throw your value away to someone who is just going to use you and then leave you. God

When you agree to a bootie call you're sacrificing yourself at the altar of THEIR betrayal--it's no way to go girl.

Now, the sex thing is an addiction. You can become addicted to people reflected in that direction.

In fact sex is the GREATEST bonder, that's why God made it that way--for the family not this guys bootie.

Now, should you do a favor/bootie call with your ex? Absolutely not--this is your greatest hex.

Why would you ever have sex with your ex? That was a failed relationship, you broke up you slut.

If an ex keeps pestering you, move away. I relocated and instantly got my life back, I remember the day.

Instead of caving in to him--again--and suffering afterwards, go to the beach/gym/call a friend.

FRENEMIES ARE ALL AROUND

Funny how people you thought were friends turn out to have fangs. They were frenemies all along, wow.

I see women giving into men sexually--lacking assertion, morals or just cuz they think they should.

Deal with the pain in your heart about this person who's betrayed you. You wanna sleep with your enemy girl?

Each time I gave in I felt in the bottom of a well in the lowest part of hell after discarded as an empty shell.

They love having you available at their convenience. They love using you as a free store or a piece.

He can just call you anytime and you're on the spot--how demeaning for you tho' he thinks he's hot.

SEX? No way, delete, block. And any time this happened, forgive yourself for you just wanted love.

It's absolutely unequal and if both parties aren't equally vulnerable it's a sick relationship pal.

They never complained when he was a pervert, they only did when he "offended"/brought someone to tears.

Toxic femininity and the women's marches celebrate their hatred for men, not their love for women.

If you've had an attachment injury the trauma energy can easily travel into the biological drives: food or sex.

The attachment injury brings constant anxiety which is only quieted by food or sex, though only temporarily.

So I became a celibate fastarian and it was all solved eventually. Ha Ha actually self-discipline is key.

REPETITION COMPULSION

A huge block develops around the repetition compulsion--the drive. Making gold on that makes you sky high.

They call telling the truth "slut shaming".

Abused children tend to grow up codependent and get involved with narcissists seeing em as compliant.

If you see these symptoms you'll know to limit contact with those types--this is gonna change your soul-height.

Narcissists are tricky: they do love-bombing/wear masks--but their symptoms are obvious besides all that.

Narcs are flimsy--they don't have a strong foundation or a self of self--only a false self, which you can tell.

He LIVES in this image he projects to others. He feels invisible like he doesn't exist if not a faker.

He was addicted like heroine to attention from others so when I wouldn't let him in it was like a siren.

They will call you "rude" for not inviting them in--but they're the rude ones for imposing/expecting it.

There's no loyalty with the narcissist, to anyone even you. Looking good to others is all they care about too.

They would rather look good to others than be happy and look good to themselves. This never works.

GOES ALONG WITH THE OTHERS
Let's say the narc likes you then asks his friends and they don't--he'll go with them rather than what he wants.

If you have a narc friend it's easy to make him turn against his partner, just say something negative.

Since they don't have a self they don't have a real opinion and will just slide in with whoever's around.

They'll always take the majority view so if you're a free thinker they'll turn against you.

Narcs are not all Don Juans or vixens. They just want supply in relationships but it's not always evident.

Gaslighting the BLACK WIDOW

The flimsy narc can't hold on to any contrary opinions if surrounded by the general narrative--weaklings.

If you're not impressed, they don't like you. If you don't like who they like, they don't like them.

They can be so impressed with someone but if you're not impressed, they're suddenly not impressed.

That's why you can't rely on narcissists: their opinions about you/themselves change: that's a constant.

They go along with the WHIMS of the crowd watching them, and that's how they fall suddenly ma'am.

He loves the girl with red hair. His friend doesn't like red hair so he begins to mull it over and question HER.

They stand on sand. What they're standing on is the opinion of others which shift with the winds.

He doesn't take into account your values, beauty or brains but others' opinions, and it's very frustrating.

DOES HE WANT YOU OR WANT TO KEEP YOU

Does he just want you--or would he do anything in the world to KEEP you? See the difference or be blue.

Nothing crazier than being in a relationship with one who's constantly changing cuza what "they're" thinking.

They may get dogmatic with religion but if no one's looking throw a curve ball. Being seen is the ALL.

If its ALL in the name of looking good to others, you can't trust em or anything they say--it's just a bother.

They don't exist to themselves--only how they look to others--so they don't exist at all, let em go.

Gaslighting the BLACK WIDOW

If you're only seen in the eyes of others, if unnoticed then you don't exist. What a painful way to live!

When a narcissist was loved but is now unnoticed, he goes into Narcissistic Rage--he blows his top, pissed.

What could be more flimsy--if he's not seen as he wants to be seen he goes into a rage. He's in his own cage.

The narcissist must always be seen on the "right side". He can't stand on his own as a hero or guide.

When his friends put down the person he's dating, he will literally GO AFTER that person suddenly.

What a weird experience to be with someone that flimsy, doing whatever others tell him to do--how silly.

In some warped way I thought he loved me cuz he tried to commit suicide over losing me. betrayed wife

OUTER DIRECTIONS

"I've never met a woman so beautiful in/out and smart, if I can't have you I don't want anybody" he said.

We're all other-directed until we're not. Groupthink dominates until we mature intellectually a lot.

Liberals wanna quibble over when life begins but the decent conservative just says: it's a baby man.

I've been in this position: the dynamics of SICK SYSTEMS and it's insanity-producing with friends flippin'

I couldn't trust anyone in my system cuz they all went on his side, the best social manipulator bringing divide.

The devil brings you down through divorce but also all the ancillary shifts in the system with everyone else.

Gaslighting the BLACK WIDOW

He had built-up resentments so when surrounded by my enemies switched to their sentiments about me.

He didn't have his own reality at all, no foundation. When they hated me, he did too without causation.

Although they're just babies in big men's bodies you still gotta get restraining orders with any gang of boys.

I was dealing with wayward children without fathers and raised by feminist mothers/I needed protection.

I feel sorry for cats and dogs so gotta feel for adult children too but only by showing em God.

It cut decades of resentment at how they imposed on me, to see: puppies/kittens hang around too if its free.

BOUNDARIES

The greatest misery is living a life that is not your own but that's what happens when the walls come down.

Narcissists hate your boundaries cuz then they can't get in to get their supply. Develop boundaries, be happy.

Without boundaries you're tossed to and fro. A household in chaos like it was torn apart by a tornado.

Without boundaries people walk all over you--they will play games with you. They sense they can push thru.

One without boundaries is codependent because he can't be his true self and the false self is a hooked shell.

Instead of resenting boundary busters see it was no boundaries attracting em in the first place. Fresh meat

Never let this cruelian know everything you know about him. Be smart, keep it to yourself and you win.

Gaslighting the BLACK WIDOW

He just wants to denigrate and doesn't know a thing. Be a mystery--don't say what you know about him.

Just start a new life without him in it. You were smitten but fortunately caught it. He's not the ONE, know it.

You're easily smitten, we all face temptation. But you stopped in time and that's how God's decidin'

If he sees women as expendable, no big thing, unimportant and subordinate--drop the bagashit.

He denigrates womenkind to compensate feminism but what about true ladies? God calls em rubies!

You started this so go ahead, shovel some more! I can outwit/outwrite you forever, you're not so clever.

Since I pity cats/dogs I should pity him too cuz I know what he went thru, but he could break me in two.

Drop the bagashit who thinks he's so important. This is the narcissist who invades your sweet reality and is a nut.

I'll do anything to escape your pomposities. A know it all peppered with sex cliches of your debaucheries.
Youtube is filled with simpleminded fools thinking they're God's tools cuz they make so much money too.

You're not like that--silly and puerile--so just stick to your humble tasks until suddenly you're in style.

FLIP-FLOPS AND STING-SHOTS

Warm and compassionate sometimes, he is capable of great cruelty when it suits him--he has two sides.

She sucked the soul right outa me. I lost my audacity as they would say. Nerve, boldness went away.

Gaslighting the BLACK WIDOW

A crappy housewife with dishes piled up is light years from a classy lady who is neat without a lot of stuff.

Narcissists are incapable of validating child's feelings since children are seen as an extension of themselves.

Her self-starvation from scapegoat syndrome paradoxically made her healthy, free of the soy problems.

Invalidation: You're too sensitive. Why are you so angry? Why can't you get along, you're just bad.

Why are you so mad about this? Why does this bother you? You're strange/can't conform too.

"You shouldn't feel that way": telling a person their feelings are invalid or even what they should be interested in.

Narcissists use invalidation to create self-doubt in their target. It sucks the life outa you, I can attest to that.

Devaluate the target to make em ready to give narcissistic supply--wow that's deep but right-on about this guy.

DEVALUATION IS SUBTLE

I can feel devaluation which is so subtle and artful I woulda missed it before-- but not today, now I'm aware.

The narc's power STEMS from invalidating you. As smitten as he is at first, get ready for a flip-flop in the stew.

"Boring as hell" cuz hell is boring and heaven is exciting. Hell is dirty disorder while heaven is purity.

A person who is self-validating will not be prey to a narcissist--we know who we are vs. a bagashit.

Feeling minimized: What do you walk away with after being in his presence? This is key despite his praises.

Gaslighting the BLACK WIDOW

If a man doesn't love me only, forget it--I know who I am and won't ever think of em again. Melania Trump

I got my Ph.D. in the Streets in Borrego Springs living without a fence and invaded by the dense.

To be invalidated by a man who should be valuing you as rubies is truly humiliating/intolerable to a queen.

Here's this guy twice her size and invulnerable, putting down a little lady who is above the rabble.

Say it sweetie: I won't be the narc's fresh meat. Things always turn cuz it's about his supply--will you meet?

Good leaders defend/protect the weaker elements--women, kids, pets. Bad leaders couldn't care less.

A 200 lb. man putting down a 100 lb. woman--how low can you go Joe, get some class hick or please go.

You being with a narc shows invalidation as a child. It's as sure as math so wake up and see the guy.

CAN'T INVALIDATE THE VALIDATED

It's a relief to know you can't be invalidated lest you're already self-invalidated. If not, you'll rise up.

You must have a question about yourself before someone else can call you into question. Jenna Ryan

The narc wants control and this how: invalidating you which is the same as saying DEVALUING you.

It's relieving that we can't be devalued unless we already agree. It won't happen save a drinking spree.

Once you know your own feelings are valid, no one can question them and this hellish curse is at an end.

Gaslighting the BLACK WIDOW

The narc has a sixth sense about an invalidated "shamed" core. I felt that way for years and was a sucker.

SHAME takes the place of invalidation. It comes second and steers the life from then on.

They want you to question your feelings or anything about yourself. It's humiliating buddy, get a life.

They want you to DISTRUST your own intuition. A raised eyebrow, rolling eyes, looking to heaven.

If a child is upset a healthy parent asks what's wrong. She validates feelings cuz she's a validated person.

One common form of invalidation is "toxic positivity" which is so phony it strip the victim of his true reality.

Lesson: Validating a child's feelings helps them to turn within to their OWN internal guidance system.

Having contact with his own core guidance system makes the child feel competent, worthy and valid.

VALIDATED CHILDREN ARE INDEPENDENT

The validated child becomes independent, going out to the world individuated, self-protected, action oriented.

When an unhealthy parent uses the child [parentifies] as an extension of herself, his life is hell.

NOTICE the subtle ways he invalidates. What you have in the frig, what's for dinner, how short your hair is.

The invalidate how you look, what you say, your viewpoints of the day, what you put on twitter--see it as bitter.

Invalidation is covert/overt. They may invalidate thru silent treatment or comparisons making you feel weird.

Gaslighting the BLACK WIDOW

If you haven't validated yourself you'll be alright with an invalidating man but you'll feel inferior/less than.

You may feel impervious to his devices but they seep into consciousness-- you're less than with others then.

Hard shell: The exploiter can't get into you if the hedge is your validated feelings about yourself.

Be aware and prepare for when you are invalidated. It hurts, you move on, you're done--that's all there is to it.

It takes time to learn all this and it takes more time to unlearn invalidation but I'm proof: it can be done.

I was self-invalidating so: when I met a handsome narcissist who continued the tradition it felt just like home.

I felt like I met my match, my homey soul mate--the way he'd make fun of me and jest to invalidate.

Unchecked invalidation is always followed by the big guns: abuse, cheating, betrayal, slander, having a harem.

Toxic friends are not only invalidating but dangerous as they build armies against you from being jealous.

Before the brain is mature the child must idolize the parents as God then it develops from there.
INVALIDATE TO <u>CONTROL</u>

The narc invalidates to make you meat. Never forget that lest you begin to feel down when it leaks/seeps.

Even a brief encounter with the narcissist can warp your view for weeks or months--a serious block.

There's something so invalidating, supercilious and uppity about him you just feel less-than.

Guard yourself, wait for his invalidation, have an escape ready and get back to your HOME center quickly.

You know he will invalidate since that's his only key to control, and controlling supply is all he knows.

The healed target wants nothing to do with the narc and sees him as the bagashit they all are.

To the healed target the narc has no more relevance, just another unreliable deceptive personage.

Your awareness of narc ways/devices stops him cold. He'll pass you by/search for other supply the cuckold.

SADISTIC *NICE* CREEPS

A kind of narcissistic supply is feeding off your pain. They like to ostracize you--your pain is their gain.

They like to rub things in your face. They like to make you feel envious. Does this not explain all of this?

They want you to feel less than so they can feel better than and that's their whole raison d'etre man.

Knowing the narc loves and feeds off your pain is the most vital information you can gain.

The weasel victim is one who shares his feelings too soon. You gotta be sure first or it's your funeral hon'.

Narcopaths will punch you in your weakest spot/weakest moment. Your dog died? That's a good one.

It's a selfish generation and thinking of others is a thing of the past. Most relational ills are from narcopaths.

The narc parent gets a sadistic thrill from hurting the child when they are most vulnerable and sad.

Later, the parent does the sweet-mean cycle and turns nice. The child is bewildered with this caprice.

The sadistic parent has a need/gets fed from the child's downs. Instead of stopping pain she eggs it on.

I'm sorry to tell you this, it's so sad. But such sick interactions are happening in homes across the land.

The narcopath bully sister will incite jealousy to get back at her little sibbilng cuz she's learned it from mommy.

"I'm gonna take Johnny instead of you--you gotta stay home" then she revels in cries against mom.

Mom talks behind her back to strangers about her daughter, the smear campaign is her rudder.

She repeated the sweet-mean cycle so often I felt an oddball--how'd a 5 year old know it was alcohol?

She'll give candy to all but one then get off on that one's cries of unfairness and even let it go on and on.

NARCOPATHIC SNAKE PITS

To the narcopath mother you're an extension of herself and on those days when she hates herself, watch out.

I was invaded by a snakepit of narcissists once. All their devices magnified into mischievous nuisance.

They hangout together to compare notes on the best targets--it's hell being in a system of narcissists.

Having em in my house was like being in a narc tank. I was clueless, I had so much to learn [God's spank].

A snakepit getting pleasure out of making you feel inferior and less-than--calling you ugly/fat/anything.

Gaslighting the BLACK WIDOW

In the system you feel there's a ranking system and you're down low. It's not reality just that of family foes.

My narc tank taught me I was nothing. A liar/criminal/thief--these labels were put on a child, can you imagine?

They're making you that way because your self-will is gone, you were never taught you even had one.

These people ban together and ostracize you getting the NARC THRILL that you suck and they're on top.

They get crazy envious over the silliest things. Once you survive the narcissist delusion you'll know your siblings.

The victim becomes a weasel feeling very incapable--when she's really so capable, just unknowledgeable.

I felt unworthy, though I was completely worthy. I felt I couldn't do anything, when I can do everything.

They love to fake nice, hook you then discard. They love to see you squirm, it's food for the day for the narc.

They seem psychic in the way they know they're getting to you which is why No-Contact is essential too.

HOW TO GET OVER YOUR EX

I'm writing this to save you untold pain and torture. Know the signs then have a good life free of narc manure.

These are the days when most are narcs. They don't think of others except as supply and it's dangerous waters.

It's hard getting over an ex but realize it's all for a reason--God is in your life so get ready for a new season.

Without this hard lesson of being hurt by someone less-than you wouldn't be what you're meant to be.

Gaslighting the BLACK WIDOW

Since we attract like, every relationship provides lessons about how to grow as a person--just listen.

We attract people to complete our healing process so if it was betrayal, that's what we needed to strengthen.

Stop resenting painful or humiliating lessons God put in your path--you couldn't learn any other way I guess.

God opposes the proud but gives grace to the humble. James 4:6. Remember that now.

Pride is a vulgar character flaw/deadly sin which the bible warns as preceding a great fall. Stay humble.

After a toxic breakup, rather than suffering for years take that information for your good/go forward dear.

One with low self-worth will have a much harder time with a breakup than someone whole, that's for sure.

I wish I hadn't said that/did that, if only I'd been clearer, maybe I can get him back: the mind goes black.

Maybe, maybe: Instead of doing the work of healing yourself and going on ahead, rearmed.
WHAT DID YOU LEARN?

Breakup: Hmm, what good did I get outa this relationship? That's the first question to ask and FORGET the rest.

Cuz the guy himself was Elmer Fudd--it's the broken bond [attachment stress] that peaked your interest.

You see, there are good things that you got out of it. There ARE some, come on. Concentrate on those hon'

What did you learn? That people can betray you suddenly and not to be complacent, just get ready.

This makes you stronger cuz you know human nature better. No one wants a naive girl, you're mature.

Not so trusting now--a terrible trait endangering everyone around your mate-- but discerning, and wow.

I never realized that someone who **LOOKS** so sweet and kind could actually be a sadist getting off on this.

The shock of such a nice guy cheating behind my back and talking about me like that was very beneficial in fact.

Now I can file that away for future reference/increase my wisdom centers that'll put me on top some day.

I matured when I realized just cuz someone looks or acts a certain way says nothing for who he **IS**, ok?

Let the other person go, now just focus on bettering yourself. Self-improve to be uniquely special.

Instead of endlessly pining over the ex, use **ALL** that energy to self-improve. When he comes to mind, move.

Then when the next relationship comes in you'll be smiling, healed, prepared and wise from the prior jilting.

YOUR GOAL IS TO HEAL

The goal is to **HEAL**--so you can let go and be free. Healing is how you get over your ex, so **FOCUS**.

Don't demonize your ex cuz then you're stuck in the hex. It's on you/future you wanna focus: get some class.

You were attracted to that type--that's what needs healing and now you have a chance by this triggering.

You wanna fix that dangerous template so you now want a man/woman who is true, loyal and has character.

Gaslighting the BLACK WIDOW

If a man you'll be attracted to a woman with something to give, who is generous, loyal and honoring to you.

There's so many rich, wisdom-inducing things to be learned from breakups and not staying stuck.

Lastly, STAY AWAY from the ex. Never entertain casual sex or one night stands with one who has rejected.

An ex who has ever used you for a sexual favor is the worst kind of loser and never see him again girl.

It wasn't a failed relationship if you learned something from it. Now go on and be the best because of it.

CURRENT TIMES

They are more worried about inciting minority anger than they are preserving our freedom: danger.

They flood into the United States--the cleanest, most orderly and fairest--and then hate our guts.

The loser renegade Don Lemon says he has a point of view, but not a bias. Have you ever heard a lie so obvious?

The Don Lemon fiasco whose ratings are abysmal by a guy who's so biased/illogical is the greatest news I know.

What is crony capitalism? It's collusion between BIG government and BIG business at OUR expense.

We laugh at honor then are shocked to find traitors in our midst. C. S. Lewis

HOME LIFE!

By far the most worthy use of my time is music listening, looking out the window and just being high.

The herb: It was a season I needed to keep the stoke going and keep me in the psychoactive right brain thinking.

Gaslighting the BLACK WIDOW

But I've let it all go, a new season is now. I wanna be part of the world and tell the truth as God told me how.

I asked God to remove the love/craving for the herb and slowly I began to prefer HEALTH and no lying.

And more than anything else in this world as a speaker and muckraker I wanted to stop COUGHING.

I heard a magnificent speaker who coughed for five minutes on the video, up for eternity ya know.

I don't like the edibles cuz once it's in you psychosis just happens and many go crazy or to the ER soon.

It's just over, that's all. That part of my life using pharmacucia--and here dad was a pharmacist.

I don't care if it is legal, it just isn't right to cough all night just to get high or merge with the sky.

God in heaven has a HUGE reward for me to suit my HUGE sacrifice I just told you about but forget it please.

It gave me other ways of seeing things and an attitude adjustment when overcoming, but now I'm Queen.

Divide your day. For me it's am. study and write. day: Hitchcock and housework. pm. music all night.

My new kittens love their new home. I suppose that's how those delinquent boys felt but I had to let em go.

FURTHER THOUGHTS

So there's a word for it: oversharing. Wow, I gotta work on that. No one ever listens to me I guess.

What era is it when a woman of substance isn't given a glance but they love garish, empty lowmindedness?

Gaslighting the BLACK WIDOW

It was a severe affliction--severe, 30 years. God put me through it I guess or it was my own sinful willfulness.

Everyone hated me and I had to learn to live with it. If that doesn't humble you nothing will, and it did.

A tiny liberal desert town surrounded by mountains where everyone knew everything in a gossip tyranny.

I'm trying not to remember it, a case of PTSD. God said put it ALL in a bag and throw the whole darn thing out.

WE RELOCATED HAPPILY

We relocated to get the hell away but what I learned about people fills these books about groupthink/evil.

No one talks about how LOW people can go. With a liberal mindset of anything goes, you don't wanna know.

If you can do those things you don't want to do, on the other side is greatness. David Goggins

Just go do what you know how to do. The reason we didn't was secondary gains from being a jerk/shrew.

The family scapegoat feels guilt and shame--that's a given and it serves the function to KEEP him down SO MOVE AWAY.

The Great Work: I'm peculiarly fitted for it--like we're all peculiarly fitted for something perhaps never done before but still legit.

Obscure poetry is the only way to avoid censorship nowadays cuz it's hidden in a few words by me.

There's nothing better than a mature man. Aren't we tired of immature men who act like that/think like that?

prosaic, puerile, obvious, boring, slow, duplicitous

Gaslighting the BLACK WIDOW

They go to war on little boys, putting little girls ahead. They even aggress on male dogs as if they did something bad.

Why does everyone think I'm talking about them? I'm amazed at the universality, it's hitting home.

You don't care anything about cats and dogs just gender pronouns and other ridiculous dogma.

CARE ABOUT REAL THINGS: CATS AND DOGS

My generation cared about cats and dogs--real things in life. You don't care about it you just want strife.

They do horrible things to monkeys in university laboratories but you don't care. This is war!

I won't invade your manosphere. Your reaction to feminists has generalized to all women--no RUBIES here.

Agitation from the world scene. Retreat back into home life where I shoulda been all along, cozy and warm.

The gain riches and fame for nothing, no mind and other mindless wastes of time but your time WILL COME.

I wanted success so bad I got ahead of God and entered a snake pit. It taught me a lesson: be patient!

I've had many failures on the way to success. It's always the same: thinking it was God then it's not.

YOU MUST BE NUMBER ONE NOW

Sis told me to go socialize with the girl sitting nearby. I was dismayed, I went in reverse, a fuddy duddy.

I'm queen in my own universe but thrown into a crowd it all goes in reverse like a spiritual hearse.

Gaslighting the BLACK WIDOW

You don't see me as Number One so I hereby withdraw all my attention cuz it's degrading/embarrassing/no fun.

You put me on their level throwing me into competition. I told you: superior man competes with no one.

Fact is you make me sick and to remember you I have your ugly pics but that's all Jack, I'm now fixed.

It feels good closing this cycle of strange attractions to a shackle, a trauma bond from way back ya' know.

He was a mental shackle, being sensitive to his reactions: I got bored as creativity became hidebound.

You know what human beings are capable of, so when it happens to you don't continue to deny it luv.

EARLY TRAUMAS SEEK CORRECTION

The fact is he's a little creep trying to one-up you out of pure envy but you ignored it being a sweetie.

Always throwing me into competition with others seen as better. You're pure but he's a blowhard usurper.

No matter what you come out feeling shabby around him. Avoid the sad Black Widow Spider Syndrome.

He's winging it. He's trying to look good. He has the right friends but it's fakery, not creative, not gold.

Study the Holocaust to see what people are like. Demons lurk in people's minds tho' seemingly nice.

If weak evil will flow in against you. You must be STRONG to avoid gaslighting by bullies, those few.

If you're different they'll demonize you just to maintain their insecure, stupid and illogical view.

Gaslighting the BLACK WIDOW

The narcissist psychopath always takes it too far. He over-reaches in his fetish to make you less.

Due to an early trauma I became eclipsed by him--a black cloud. Now I'm back again, will shout out loud!

DON'T BE DEMEANED BY GOING THERE

It's so demeaning to lurk with your nose pressed up the glass, the back of the class: no more, Lass.

You think after going thru all that I'm gonna put up with you too baby? No way, I'm returning to sanity.

I lived in a desert ghost town invaded by nincompoops and malcontents, I'm done with that.

Tho' the CPTSD is bad, the PTSD from that era was even worse because the memories are so fresh.

They seek to devalue you any way they can. And when you become perfect they'll call you an old man.

I've had it with the human race and all it's divisions and status-tensions, will separate as long as I can.

It's about NOT going there--to the channel or whatever. NOT doing something gets you to your future.

KNOW YOUR LIMITATIONS

You think I'm gonna overcome all that crap from the female community and now you too? NO.

Besides, there's nothing in you the narcissist anyway. It's all outer directedness seeking attention/acclaim.

You are your WHIMS I guess, whatever catches your fancy. Who'd wanna live like this anyway?

Gaslighting the BLACK WIDOW

I want stability--HOME--where I can walk tall and not feel criticized or less-than as compared to others.

HOME is my only protection against people like you. So why the hell would I seek you out and be blue?

You're not gonna get into my consciousness and ruin my day like you did yesterday. You're nipped, ok?

Don't call em filthy pigs let em implode on their own. God destroys beauty, like grass they're mowed down.

Those who are trauma-bonded must take distance by blocking him so she can TRULY see him.

CORRECTION-SEEKING//YOU DON'T LOVE HIM

NO one'd put up with this unless there be early trauma from broken bonds seeking correction.

You have no interest in the property, admit it. All you wanna do is watch TV all day, wasting it.

When asked what they hated about their husbands, 87% of the wives polled said "it's his procrastination".

Recognize your tendency to go fast-forward in a relationship like future-faking: now grow up.

The trauma-bonded grow up weirded, thinking "i'm gonna have his baby" without blinking. Slow down.

You know what it's like now to suddenly wake-up to who you're with. You don't need another big switch.

I'm for you--I don't want you to get hurt again. So slow down, get to know a person--real, real well.

If you're a neat freak and he's a bit messy, forget em, see? If you get 'r dun and he procrastinates, flee!

Gaslighting the BLACK WIDOW

Of you'll be bitchin' about the projects undone and taking the blame for a personality disorder--no fun.

I wish I could talk to you but I'll forget about that. I'll rely on the word and prayer for now, just where I sat.

He "showed an interest" in the yard for an hour but left all his snippings behind and never finished <sigh>.

EAT THEN DON'T EAT

As for what is a superior man, we leave that to your imagination cuz it's obvious wisdom.

The Old Lady Diet is smoothies, soups and dips. For digestion there's no other way to do it.

No matter what happens I have my daily trump card: the fast. Breakfast is behind me, I'm flying at last.

Why did you call me lost? There were my silent years but that's a phase of the hero's creative process.

100 KAREN KELLOCK BOOKS

AFFINITY OR MISERY
AGELESS CORNUCOPIA
AMERICA AWAKE!
AMERICA'S DAFT ERA
ARTS OF PALEO FASTING
AUTOPHAGY ON CHEATERS
BACKSTABBING NEUROTICS
BETRAYAL TRAUMA
BOOMERS AND BROKENNESS
BOOT ON NECK
CHAMPION GUIDES
COMMIE NUTHOUSE
COMMIES
COMMUNIST SPIRIT
CONTAGION OF MADNESS
CONTAGIOUS MADNESS
CULTURE CLASH BASHED
DAFT LEFT
DAILY FASTARIAN
DAM RATS
DIVERSITY IS CRUELTY
E-RACE WHITE
EVIL FREAKS (Beyond Gross)
THE END OR A BEND?
FEMALE BULLIES AND FEMI-NAZIS
FEMALE CARNALITY
FEMALE DUMB DOWN
FEMALE POWER DRIVE
FEMINISM AND RUIN 1 & 2
FIX FOR MISFITS
FOOLS & TRAMPS
FREEDOM SPEAKING
FRENEMY ENABLER
FRENEMY LIAR
FRENEMY THIEF
FRENEMY TRAITOR
TRENEMY TYRANT
GENIUS IS HELD DOWN
GLOBALISLAM
GOD USES THE FLAWED
HAZE OF THE LATTER DAYS

THE HERD IN WORDS
HIX POLITIX
HOW THEY RUINED US
JUST SKIP DINNER
LE FEMME AND THE COMMUNIST SPIRIT
LIBERAL CHAOS & ROT
LIBERAL DOUBLETHINK
LIBERAL GALL 1 & 2
LIBERAL SHOVE-DOWNS
LOCK YOUR GATE
LOSERS and Femme Fatales
MANUAL FOR SUPERIOR MEN
MODERN ART FROM HELL
MOSTLY FAKE
NOTES TO CHAMPS 1 & 2
OVERCOME FRENEMIES
PC MAKES US CRAZY
PEOPLE ARE CRUEL
PEOPLE PROBLEMS 1 & 2
PERSECUTED GENIUIS
POLI-PSYCH MYSTERIES
PRETENTIOUS SLOBS
QUEEN BEE
RED NEW DEAL
RETURNING TO FIRST NATURE
SEASON OF TREASON
SEPARATE MEANS HOLY
SOCIAL HYPNOTISM
SOLITUDE SOLUTION
SUPERCILIOUS
THE SCHOOLS SCREWED EM UP
TOAD TO PRINCE
TRIALS CYCLES
TRUMP VS. GROUP
TRUST IN TRASH
THE TRUTH ABOUT PEOPLE
UNDERHEANDEDLY CLEVER
WALK TALL WITHIN WALLS
WE'RE NOT ALL ONE
WINNERS SKIP DINNER
WORK OR SMERK

KAREN KELLOCK PH.D.

M.S. Political Science, San Diego State. Ph.D. in Psychology, University of California Irvine. Postdoctoral: UCI School of Medicine, Dept. of Psychiatry [NIMH Grants]. Developed the Debris Theory of Disease, a theory of system pathology in 120 books and 22 textbooks for the general public. The theory has a general formula: All disease is obstruction, all recovery is elimination, all success is attraction. The three obstructions are people, habit and food. Remove obstruction and snap to your goals, waiting in the wings.